BUTRINT   *AL BANIA*

History, Monuments and Museum

DHIMITËR ÇONDI

Acknowledgements

As author of this book and as one of th archaeologist and leaders of the archeological excavations and research at Butrint for more than 30 years, I feel it as an obligation to thank all my colleagues and collaborators who have given an unstinting support and contribution for this archaeological site.

Firstly, I would like to thank my professors Dhimosten Budina, Neritan Ceka, Muzafer Korkuti, Shpresa Gjongecaj, Faik Grini, Gëzim Sala, Ilir Gjipali and Iris Pojani, my colleagues Astrit Nanaj and Kosta Iako, and as well my foreign collaborators and colleagues in many projects, Richard Hodges, Sandro De Maria, kostandinos Zaho, Katerina Haxhis and Roberto Pena.

I would also like to thank all those who have given a direct contribution for the publishing of this book; Oliver Gilkes who contributed with the editing and translation in to English, Sabina Veseli, Smirald Kola, Engjell Seriani, Ibrahim Bajrami, Elio Hobdari, Gjegj Vinjau and Erjona Qilla.

Last but not least, I would like to thank all those who with their kindness to me, to archaeology and especially to Butrint, have inspired and encouraged me to publish this book.

Dhimitër Çondi

View from Mountain Mile to Kalivo, Butrint and Corfu

Map of the Epirote tribes

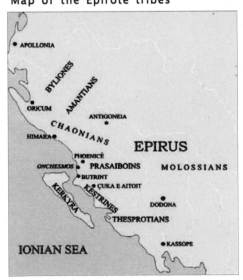

Map of the Prasaebes region

King Phyrrus (318 - 272 BC)

Butrint today

History of the City

In the southwest of Albania lies the, Ksamil or Heksamil (six miles) peninsula. A long narrow, rocky ridge, it is linked with the mainland to the north. On the western side its rugged shores rise steeply from the deep waters of the Ionian Sea, while on the eastern side from the lake of Butrint, the ancient Pelodes (the muddy harbour), or, as it was called, the lake of the nymphs.

Butrint, ancient Buthrotum, lies on the southern tip of the peninsula, virtually surrounded by the Vivari channel through which the ebb and flow of tides carry the waters of the lake to the sea. The land beyond, the Kestrina or Vrina Plain, is flat and marshy. Thus the city occupies a position well protected by nature and with a natural harbour and this is mentioned in the maritime itineraries of the ancient world. The major sea route from Dyrrachium and Aulona to Nicopolis and beyond passed via Buthrotum.

From the plain of Kestrina and the surrounding hills Butrint secured ample supplies of grain and livestock products. The lake, rich in fish and shellfish, also served as permanent reserve of food. Because of these natural conditions, a centre of habitation arose at Butrint in prehistoric times, and this centre gradually grew, took shape, increased in strength and extended in area.

By the Early Iron Age the top of the hill was home to a settlement that may have been walled. This settlement formed the embryo of the future city. Butrint is identified as a city for the first time in written sources when it was mentioned by Hecataeus, the geographer of the 6th century BC. In this time the city extended over the whole area of the hill. However, we do not encounter its name again until 500 years later. An ancient legend, revived by Teucer of Cyzicus, says that fleeing from the destruction of Troy to the west, Helenus, the son-in-law of the Trojan King Priam, sacrificed an ox to ensure his safe entry to Epirus.

The wounded ox plunged into the sea, swam into a bay and emerged on the shore of a land where he fell and died. Helens took this as a omen and called the place "Buthrotos".

The legend and the beauties of Butrint have inspired poets and writers down through the ages. Virgil devoted whole pages to it in his masterpiece the "Aeneid", recounting the voyage of another Trijan hero. The events in Racine's "Andromaque", also, take place at Butrint. Stripping away the myth though we are left with the truth that Butrint became a significant city, one of the most important indeed in the region of Epirus, and the tribal city of the Chaonians.

With the passage of time the city expanded. In the 4th century BC, much of the city centre, including the circuit walls, temples and shrines to Asclepius the healing god were built and it began to spread outside the defensive circuit. At the end of that century, as if to mark its importance, a territorial boundry wall was erected across the peninsula at the place called Dema, to the north. Thus, the whole territory of the peninsula became directly dependent on the city.

After 168 BC, when the polity of the Praesebes was formed, centered on Butrint, but carved out of the old Chaonia as part of the Epirote League, the life of the city assumed a further impetus. Butrint became the main centre of this territory, with a number of tributary cities and settlements (Karalibeu, Qenurio, "Kalivona", Vagalat, Malathreno, Cuka e Ajtoit, Kataajnon). As a series of inscriptions show the city had its own po;ocy, such as the making of peace and war, administered its revenues and arranged treaties, and enacted new laws. It also had a full series of civic institutions, ranging from a number of councils, through the *strategoi*, its military commanders, and a civil head of the league, the prostates, the head of the executive power, and the chief priest of the whole tribe. The archaeological evidence for this stage of the citys life clearly reflects this strengthening of the city. Two temples and the theatre testify to its increasing cultural needs. The southern defensive wall, which further extended the area of the city, also belongs to this period. What is more important, however, is the fact that this added area belongs to the cultural centre, the theatre, the temples and the *agora* or central square.

As long as Butrint remained within framework of the Epirote League it followed the same political course as Phoenice, the main centre of this league, just 25 km away at the head of the lake. Thus, Butrint, like Phoenice did not share in the fate of the 70 other cities of Epirus, which were destroyed by the Romans following their conquest of Macedonia. After the breakup of the Epirote League, Butrint retained its rights as the main centre of the region. Moreover, at this period the importance of Butrint increasingly overshadowed that of Phoenice, which gradually declined.

The interests of Rome in this zone emerged early. We learn this from the historian Polybius, who writes about the presence there of merchants from Italy. What attracted the Roman Empire especially were the natural resources of the country, its favourable position as a commercial centre accessible by land and sea, as well as its fine strategic position as a naval base where any fleet could anchor safely. Butrint, was established as a Roman colony in the later part of this period, the first attempt being made by Julius Caesar in 44BC. However a functioning colony was not actually created until the time of Emperoro Augustus at the very end of the first century BC. The city was remodelled with a constitution and recived an influx of colonisits fro Italy even though the number of local population was dominant. Initially Latin seems to hae been used extensively, certainly for official inscriptions, though by the 2–3rd centuries BC of 21 names known from inscriptions, only six were Italic.

One element of the new city was its expansion across the Vivari Channel typified by the building of an aqueduct to supply the town with water from the Xarra springs, probably via a bridge over the channel. The aqueduct, about three km long is depicted in some of Butrint's coins of the periods of

Augustus and Nero. The city was extended onto the Vrina plain and was subject of new building activities. Later the theatre was reconstructed; a very large number of baths, public and private, the gymnasium and three nymphea were built.

Following a probable earthquake in the 3rd century AD the city centre was largely abandoned, its staues broken and overturned and civic buildings abandoned. However, reconstruction occurred in the later 4th century AD, the public baths and the gymnasium were decorated with mosaics. This was may be connected with the reign of Julian Apostates who encouraged the construction of public buildings in Epirus. Later on Christianity was introduced, Butrint having its own martyr in St. Terinus, who was slain during the regin of the mid 3rd centry Emperor Trajan Decius. Nevertheless bar a possible martyr shrien by the channel there is little evidnce of any major religious buildings and the first mention of a bishop only occurs in the 451 year AD, under the authority of the episcopate of Nikopolis.

During late antiquity period the city underwent further changes typical of the period, with a reduction of settlement and an emphasis on a townscape domiated by churches, other religious buildings and large private dwellings. A new fortification wall was built extending all around the channelside, possibly in reaction to incursions of seasbonr Vandals or oerhaps the Ostrogoths uder King Totila, who in 551, conquered Corfu, the Subote islands and the near by Onchesmos (Saranda).

Butrint was still an important centre during the early medieval period. It was mentioned as an important town, initially from George of Cyprus and Arsenios of Corfu (876–953) who highlighted the importance of the lands, the forests, and the richness of the lake with fish and mussels, all elements that were to recur over the following centuries. Archaeologically there is little aterial fort his toime, buildings were largely of timber, and the town was in any case much reduced in size. However, the fortifications appear to have remained in use and were attacked at least once in the early middle ages to judges for the burnt debris witin the towers of the western walls.

Reorganisation and rebuilding seems to have occurred during the mid Byzantine period, a local administrative centre was established at a rebuilt church complex on the Vrina Plain, lead seals of official despatches from a number of Byzantine officials, including a eunuch of the sacred bedchamber in Constantinople, have been found. A symptom of its revival is the renewed strategic interest in Butrint, between 1081 and 1084 it was the scene of conflict between the Byzantine Empire and the expansive Norman state established in southern Italy. Butrint was mentioned by the Arab geographer Al–Idriz in the 12th century in «Qitabi Rozherin», as a small town, but with a considerable population, and large markets. Some evidence of these has come to light in the form of numerous coins. In 1204 after the fourth crusade shattered the Byzantine Empire, Butrint fell into the sphere of interest of the Despotate of Epirus, though it changed habds fairly frequently as the fronteit in the Balkans swayed back anf forth between crusader states, Byzantines,

Epirote and the new Italian poer, the Angevin French. Finally in 1386 it purchased by the Republic of Vencie as part of a deal whereby they acquired Corfu from the Angevins to use as a fortress in their long-runing war with Republic of Genoa. The city has lost its grandeur but maintained its importance as a strategic point in the Vivari channel controlling rich fisheries, and of course became a bastion in its own right against the expanding power of the Ottoman Turks who overthrew the last Byzantine powers and conquered mostof the Balkans in the 15th nad 16th centuries. Major Turkish armies were based there in 1537, uner Sultan Suleiman the Magnificent and again in 1716 under Sultan Achmet III during the two failed Turkish attemts to capture Corfu. Butrint was taken by the Napoleonic French in 1796 following Napoelons overthrowof the Venetian Republic but was quickly I turn seized by Ali Pasha Tepelena, who in 1807 built the castle at the mouth of the Vivari Channel to prevent its reconquest from the west. As a result of systematic excavations the importance of Butrint is revealed, making the ancient town an important centre of Albania's archaeological heritage attracting local and foreign visitors. From 1992, Butrint was listed as a world heritage site by UNESCO, and has been attracting the interest of researchers and donators from all over the world.

Maps showing the earliest wall circuits

Butrint acropolis cyclopean wall

Dema wall on the shore line

Excavation
in Butrint

Monuments at Butrint

The Fortification

The hill of Butirnt is not very big. It is comprised of limestone formations, covered with a hard layer of soil. On the south side, a rampart of rock rises vertically from the flat below, while the other sides for the most part fall away steeply to the edge of the lake. On the west side alone, a narrow isthmus which broadens into the flat links the hill with the remainder of the peninsula. At the beginning, or perhaps, in the middle of the Early Iron Age the plateau on top of the hill may have had a defensive wall. It was built of large blocks of stone with the edges broken so they would fit together better. It was partly rebuilt later, in the 1st century BC, the Blocks used in this reconstruction are large (about 2x1 m) and heavy (4-5 tons), but carefully hewn. The faces are flat while the blocks have regular polygonal form. For better defence the former straight line of the walls is interrupted with buttresses and embrasures. The abundance and the richness of the archaeological material, the imports from Corfu and Kerkyra, found here, provide excellent evidence for the importance of the town in the archaic period.

One century later Butrint had extended over the whole five hectares of the hill perhaps with a new circuit wall on the lower slopes of the hill.

The four surviving gates belong to this period of construction and the development of the city. The Lion Gate and the Lake Gate are the best preserved. The development of the city and its further extension to the south, at the beginning of the 3rd century BC, made necessary the construction, on the flat, of a new wall which extended the area of the city. This wall, built of rectangular blocks hewn to the some height, encloses the area of the shrine of Asclepius and theatre, the agora and continues to the double-towered Hellenisitic tower gate.

This is an impressive doube entrance portal with one square tower and a larger eastern tower with a semi-circular end. On the outer face, there was a drop door which could be closed quickly to block the entry of attackers and possibly trap them.

In the 1st century BC, another tower was erected, and parts of the wall were restored, also with large rectangular blocks but now fixed with mortar.

Late Antique defences dating from the 4th -6th centuries are the most numerous of the later walls. In these tempestuous centuries full of attacks and invasions, the whole citcuit wall was rebuilt, with a new outer addition along the southern side of the city, following the Vivari Channel. Moreover, at this time the former barrier at Dema, was reinforced with a new curtain and watchtowers.

The construction, reconstruction and reinforcement of walls went on throughout the Middle Ages, up to the 16th century when the city was finally abandoned. At this time the length of the wall exceeded 2.5 km, enclosing an area of 16 hectares. It followed the edge of the lake and the Vivari channel. At this period, too, the old acropolis on the top of the hill was restored as a castle dominating the small township on the low lying land below.

In the defence structures crossed the boundary of the Vivari channel. Opposite Butrint a fortress was built, probably in the 16th century or perhaps earlier, at first simply a triangle of walls, to which the towers and other structures were added in the 16th and 17th centuries. This worked in tandem with a square blockhouse on the northern shore and the two together protected the fish wier that ran across the channel between them. These new defences at first supplemented but later replaced Butrint's older wass and ultimately the triangular fortress became the focal pint of Butrint. Finally, in 1807, at the outlet of the Vivari channel, Ali Pasha Tepelena built the last fortress erected to defend the site. This was a small square fort, bult using an earlier fortified go=house as a core, with artillery bastions to dominate the anchorage in Butirnt bay.

Wall fragment, 6th century BC

Maps showing Hellenistic wall circuits

Ancient
parallelepiped
wall, 4th – 3rd
century BC

Ancient
polygonal
wall,
4th – 3rd
century BC

Map of late
Roman and
late Roman
Butrint

Roman construction
near ancient walls

Tower of western defense wall

Late antiquity wall

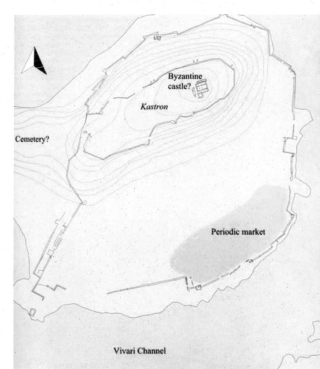

Medieval proteichisma wall at the western defenses

Map of medieval wall fortifications

The Water Gate

Medieval waterfront wall

Aerial view of the Triangular castle

The watch tower

Ali Pasha's castle

The Venetian tower by the Vivari channel

The city gates

The southern gate (opposite the theatre)
It is of a frontal type gate, built straight itnot eh city wall at this point. This entrance was significant as it was the chief means by which pilgrims tot eh shrine of Asclepius would have eneteed the city and it may have been retained long after the wall had ceased to be of any importance for ritual purposes.

The tower gate
This fine Hellenistic gate has two towers, a square western tower and a round ended eastern bastion. The eastern tower was so designed to flank any possible attackers on their shieldless sie. There were originally two gates one to the side of either tower, and both towers seem to have had at least two floors. This impressoive structure remained in use well into the Roman period where it was left to provide a monumental entrance into the city interior.

The Scean Gate or Lake Gate
Set into the Hellenistic wall line is a substantial gateway pf the 4th centry BC, the Lake Gate. While much of the wall on this side of the city has collapsed and been rebuilt, this fine corbelled archway has survived, an original feature of the Hellenistic defensive circuit that gives access to a stairway and path leading up to the summit of the acropolis. The paving in the sloping gate tunnel and pivot blocks for the doors appear to be medieval.

The gateway was discovered and excavated by the Italian Archaeological Mission of the 1920s and 30s, and became a centrepiece of Italian and Fascist party propaganda, being interpreted as evidence of the truth of the Virgilian legend. The excavator, Luigi Maria Ugolini, named it the Scaean Gate after the great portal in Troy, the miniature copy of which was supposedly seen by Aeneas at Butrint. As part of celebrations for the 2000th anniversary of Virgil's birth in 1931, a commemorative postage stamp was issued showing King Helenus standing in the gateway, presenting a sharp fascist salute to Aeneas arriving by ship.

The Lion Gate
The Lion Gate, dating to the 4th century BC, is named after the impressive carving of a lion attacking a bull that decorates the great lintel. The bull lies on the ground, and only its horns and head are visible. The carving of the lion is somewhat eroded and, as can be seen from the carving of the tail, it may never have been fully completed. The original gateway here was another Hellenistic corbelled archway, larger than the Lake Gate. This structure has been partly hidden by rebuilding of medieval date, when a

tower was added to the re-entrant angle of the wall here. The lion relief was reused as an element of the door that led into the city. Originally the sculpture probably decorated the Hellenistic gate; if so, the Archaic style of the relief suggest that it was reused from an earlier gate, possibly from the acropolis. sitting on top of the wall above as a typical gate sculpture.

The northern gate
This is accessed by a rmap up the northern side of the city and originally swung in through the walls onto a presumably stepped pathway. Its original build dates to the 4th centry BC but it was clearly reconsturcted and maintained as functioning gate until into the Middle Ages

The western gate
Ths has been considerably altered over time, and was exacavted to provide an access way for the light railway system of the Italian Archaoelogcal Misison of the 1920s and 30s. It is a conventional gateway that orirginally would have lheld a double leaved door giving access to the interior of the walls here. Later int eh Middle Ages, it worled together with other walls and gates to provide a well-protected approach to the castle on the acropolis.

Map of the Hellenistic gates

The southern gate (opposite the theater)

Tower Gate *(reconstruction)*

The tower gate

The Scean Gate or Lake Gate

The Lion Gate

The western gate

The northern gate

The Shrine of Asclepius and the City Centre

The cultural centre of Butrint developed in the space between the rock and the encircling wall. At first it com-prised the promenade and the temple of Asclepius. Later, the theatre was built on a new temple above the theatre, shorten-ing the promenade.

The monuments which comprise the centre, the promenade, the temples and the theatre, were built as separate entities of massive blocks of stone. The whole achieves a striking harmony of composition through the care-ful distribution of the different structures of varying propor-tions, which blend with the natural background. In the first centuries of our era the centre underwent no radical alter-ation.

During these centuries, the stage of the theatre and the lower temple were reconstructed according to the require-ments of the time, but the complete retention of the existing limits and volumes prevented any alteration in the overall form of the square. The only new construction at this time was the main public bath of the city.

Here is the shrine of Asclepius, demarcated to the south by the large block-built wall of the 3rd or 4th century BC, which acted both as an early line of the city defences and as the *temenos* of the sacred area. The actual temple of Asclepius is up on the side of the acropolis, behind the theatre. It is a small prostyle temple, probably of the Ionic order, with a cella with a mosaic pavement perhaps of 3rd century BC date.

The size and form of the temple are typical of Epirote temples. Behind the city wall and to the left is a tangle of walls ranging in date from the Hellenistic era to Late Antiquity. The original phase here, consisting of a small building with an inner courtyard, is interpreted as a *prytaneum*.

Passing down the slope, we pass the remains of an outer gateway, past the piers of a Roman arch and through the original gateway in the Hellenistic wall. This opens into an irregular stone-paved area, with the *prytaneum*, a municipal hospitality hall, at its west end. Today it is flooded with groundwater, evidence of the tectonic changes in the area, and the visitor is restricted to the wooden walkway. The piazza has a stone pavement that was a gift of one of its citizens, a freedman called Gnaius Domitius Eros, who included his name in lead letters set into the marble pavement in front of the *prytaneum*.

All around the sides were small shrines, treasuries, dedicatory stelae and statue bases, while a brick-built cleansing fountain stood on the north side. This was the public entrance into the theatre.

From here a path led round the back of the treasury of Asclepius, via a stepped *vomitorium*, directly into the *cavea* of the theatre. Another entranceway led through the *parodos*, between the *cavea* and *scena*, and into the orchestra. Taking this second route we pass by the doorway and windows of a treasury building. The structure here is a Roman reconstruction

Central Butrint showing the forum

of the Hellenistic original on the same spot. Long believed to have been the temple of Asclepius, it is clear that while this vaulted room functioned as a shrine, focused on a natural cleft in the rock at the back (the *favissa*, which was accessed through a window that began as a possible healing well), it is not the main temple. Instead, it was here that pilgrims made their offerings to the priests of the cult, placing money into a massive stone moneybox that stands within the inner door. By the Roman period the interior was packed with valuable objects and precious instruments sacred to the cult, kept safely under lock and key.

A further indication of the public nature of this area is the large number of inscriptions in Greek carved into the north side of the *parodos* wall. These all date to between the later 3rd and later 1st centuries BC, to a time when the city was clearly flourishing. They record ceremonies that occurred in the theatre, namely the manumission or freeing of groups and families of slaves by their masters, a conspicuous act of largesse dedicated to Asclepius and sometimes to another important local deity, Zeus Soter.

Inscriptions such as this give us the names of slaves, their owners (who might unusually be women) and the priests and magistrates of the city who officiated. This drives home the point that the theatre was not merely a venue for entertainment but also a focus for communal worship and political meetings. Indeed, entertainment, religion and politics might merge together without conflict.

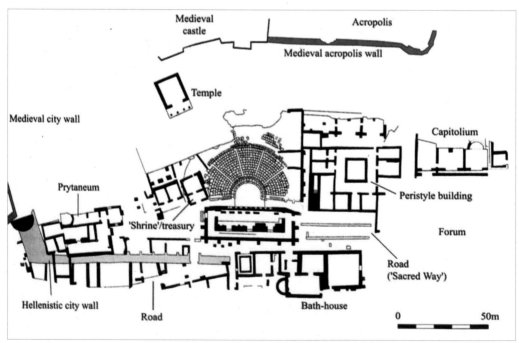

Plan of the agora of Butrint

The Asclepian treasury

Head of Asclepius

The temple of
Asclepius

Prytaneum

The Roman Fountain

The parados of the theater, showing manumissions.
A manumission (slave freedom decree)

The Theatre

The theatre at Butrint seems to have been a creation of the 3rd century BC, possibly under King Pyrrhus (306–272 BC), who carried out an active building programme throughout his kingdom The *cavea*, or seating banks, are cut into the hillside in the Greek fashion, and retained on the east and west by block-built *analemma* walls. The seats are divided into upper and lower sections by a semi-circular walkway, the *diazoma*. There are five sections, or *cunei*, divided by stairs seating around 1500 spectators. A now virtually illegible dedicatory inscription may be seen on the third row of seats, and other manumission inscriptions are carved on blocks on the *diazoma*. The lower rows of seats are the *proedroi*, or seats of honour for magistrates and leading citizens; they are carved as benches with lion-feet terminals. Cuts and holes into the stone of the seats indicate the later addition of tribunals and awnings to cover the auditorium. The entire *cavea* was massively enlarged by the Romans, probably at the end of the 2nd century AD, and new rows of seats were built over the treasury of Asclepius and on buttresses to the east.

The stone-paved orchestra was the focal point of the Hellenistic theatre; this area is now underwater and covered by the modern stage. To the south of the orchestra stood the *scena* building and stage. In the original structure this was probably a relatively small building. However, with the 2nd-century reconstruction of much of the complex, the *scena* was completely rebuilt as a large two-storied *scena frons*, with architectural elaboration and marble veneer. Three doorways, the central *valva regia* and the flanking *valvae hospitales*, permitted the actors to move around the stage building; these entrances were flanked with intercolumnar stone-built podia with niches for small sculptures. The stage was also restructured, underlining the greater emphasis placed by the Romans on this feature. Though it cannot now be seen, the edge of the stage has a slot to hold a curtain, which following ancient practice was hauled upwards, rather than let down.

During the excavations of the 1930s, a large group of sculptures was found on the stage, in various stages of being broken up. This was probably happening after the abandonment of the theatre in Late Antiquity, and was a common practice at this time: marble was broken up and burnt down to produce high-quality lime to make mortar. Many of the statues may have decorated the auditorium or adjacent spaces. The group included fine portraits of Augustus, his wife Livia, and the great general Marcus Vipsanius Agrippa, the victor of the battle of Actium. Another sculpture, which came to be known as the 'Goddess of Butrint', in fact depicts the god Apollo (Augustus' patron deity).

On the eastern side of the theatre, and joined to it by a staircase and private entrance to the other *parodos*, is the so-called peristyle building. This may have acted as the headquarters of the cult, the place where the priests kept their vestments, sacred vessels and records, and where the private ceremonies and banquets that were part and parcel of the worship could occur. It was originally two storied, a surviving staircase also leads into the theatre. A series of rooms were arranged around an central stone flagged courtyard, while an entrance passage led off to the roadway to the south with convenient benches for the servants of visitors. Other than its obvious ink tot eh cult of Asclepius it is a typical dwelling from the Hellenistic world.

Columnar tripod base in the western parados

The excavated theater in 1932 with the view over Vivari channel to the Butrint plain beyond

View of the theater at Butrint

Roman scena of
the theater

Axonometric
reconstruction of
the stage building, by
Carlo Ceschi

A peristyle house and its plan, 2ⁿᵈ century AD

Stoa, 4ᵗʰ century BC

Byzantine church, 13ᵗʰ century
AD panel of painted plaster

Plan of the area of the Forum and the tripartite building, showing the find spot of the monumental togate statues

Roman forum

Statue of Augustus

The Gymnasium

This is an enigmatic complex dating to the 1st or 2nd centuries AD. A brick fountain forms the centerpiece dividing it into two halves. The fountain has mosaics of water birds and a *kantharos* bowl at the top of the nices. The whole was originally plastered and veneered in marble, and lead pipes brought water up to the niches from where it would have flowed into the basin. but its original purpose is unknown. The two spaces to either side of the fountain, and adjacent rooms are paved with mosaics. It was converted to a church in the middle ages and the inscription now lying in the pool was used as the altar. It is certainly not a gymnasium in the Hellenisitic sense, but the resecne of the brick fountain certainly denotes it as a public facility. It moight possibly have been a library or perhaps ws another religious complex. Adjacent to the 'Gymnasium' is a square stone monument, originally covered with stone slabs, with a doorless vaulted chamber. While similar in form to a tomb it may be that this is a cenotaph or *heroon*, a shrine to a hero, perhaps commemorating an illustrious figure associated with Butrint's ancient origins.

The Inscription Tower

The tower was built of 105 stone inscriptions in Greek, which are mainly manumission decrees, freeing slaves, similar to those int the theatre. The inscriptions contain the name of the slave and the witnesses during the release ceremony. They are dated from 157 BC when the Praesebes *Koinon* was independent until 44–31 BC, when the Roman Colony at Butrint was established. These inscriptions had been reused in a tower of the city wall and have been rebuilt here as a wall for public display.

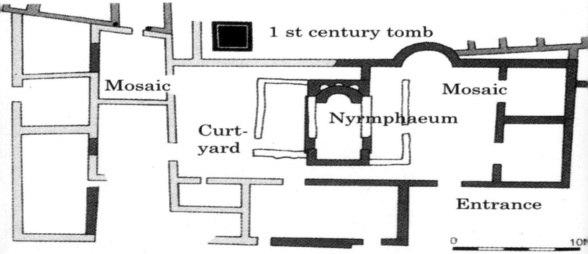

Gymnasium and its plan

View of the Gymnasium, 1st –2nd century AD

Nympheum into the gymnasium

Aerial view of the Gymnasium

The Inscription Tower   Inscription

A tomb

Nympheum and wells

There were three monumental fountains, nympheums, two of them large and one small, in Butrint. The main nym-pheum comprises the water reservoir, a small chamber from which water was taken, and the nympheum proper, with the basin and arched wall with niches for statues. In front the edge of the basin is straight, while at the back it is semi-circular in shape. Above it runs the wall with three niches. They are linked with one another and with the reservoir by a channel running behind them. The water flowed through them into the basin.

On its outer surface the nympheum was covered with thin slabs of white marble, while the inside with multicolored marble. Marble statues, dedicated to gods, occupied the niches of the nympheum. The outer layer of white marble gave the nympheum a transparency which was further enhanced by the water flowing over it, Its main parts, the basin, the wall with the statues, emphasized by the multicoloured marble facing, harmonized the movement of the water with the immobility of the statues.

The Nympheum, built during 1st–2nd century AD, was part of the aqueduct system of the town built in the Augustian period, of a length of three kilometres and the source of the water was probably a spring of Xarra. The line of its brick-built piers stand across the Vrina Plain and in front of the Tower Gate in Butrint.

Nympheum

It has the shape of a niche, constructed with bricks, plastered, and a quadrangular basin which was supplied with water from the aqueduct. It is of a height of 2m, and it is dated in the 2nd century AD.

The Well of Nymphs

Passing under the gate one enters a small stepped piazza. Located off to the left, down a short flight of steps, is the Well of Junia Rufina. At one time a freshwater spring, the well has a natural grotto-like appearance that must have enhanced its appeal as a sacred well. Certainly offerings were placed into its waters from about the 4th century BC. In the Roman period it was elaborated with a wellhead, and the stone balustrade was carved with an inscription: *Junia Rufina friend of the nymphs* [built this].

In the 5th or 6th century the pagan well was Christianised with the addition of a painting on the back wall. In this painting two peacocks flank a *kantharos* cup, the same symbols of paradise and everlasting life seen in the Baptistery. Though now much weathered and faded, the right-hand peacock can still just be seen near the niche.

In the Middle Ages the well was walled up and a hole cut in the roof so that the castle garrison could draw water. A series of chapels were erected from the 5th century at the head of the steps creating a church on multiple levels ending at the well. Pilgrims would be able to descend through a series of stages to the crypt-like space at the bottom. The upper doorway is still visible in the western wall. A cemetery with late antique and medieval graves was located around the uppermost chapel. The old well space became a crypt where offerings continued to be made in the wall niche. Even after the chapel was ruined this practice continued. Ugolini, the Italian archaeologist who opened up and excavated the well, recorded that fishermen left offerings here in the 1920s, and even today women from local villages will come to make gifts to Junia Rufina in the hope that they will be granted healthy families.

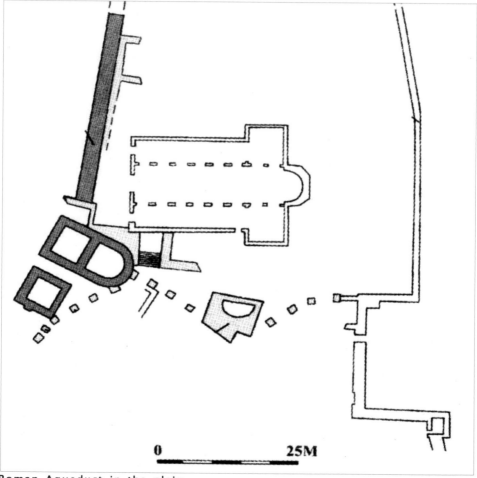

Roman Aqueduct in the plain

Nympheum 2nd century AD. Statues found in the nympheum (Dionysius and Apollo)

Roman nympheum behind the Inscription Tower

Roman coin with the aqueduct

Roman Aqueduct in the Vrina Plain

Aqueduct in the city

Fragment from the viaduct
on the Vivari channel

The well of Nymphs of the Junia Rufina

Epicoco's painting of the Junia Rufina fresco

The Public Baths

The baths of Butrint are to be found all over the city and its subuirbs. A total of 14 public and provate bathhouses are known.

The bath by the theatre is undoubtedly one of the major public baths of the city and is likely to have been connected with the shrine of Asclepius. It was erectedin the later 2nd century AD, replaceing an earlier complex. Only a portion of it has been excavated including the entrance, apodyterium, or undressing room, a public latrine and one of the major hot rooms with a suspended floor and semi-circular plubge bath.

A further bathhouse is situated next tot eh Venetian blockhouse by the Vivari channel. This is more likely to be a private bath belongin to a large house complex. A hexagonal central room, originally roofed with a cupola, has on its southern side heated rooms and on the other by cold plunge baths. .

In the third bath, that near the baptistery, two heated chambers, placed one after the other, have been uncovered. Under the floors of these chambers ran ceramic pipes, with lateral perforations to facilitate the circulation of gasses, During the archaeological excavations, a votive inscription dedicated to Zeus Cassios, the god protecting mariners, was discovered, This may indicate that this bath was for mariners, a thing that shows the importance of Butrint as a port.

Fially the largest bathhouse of the city is the least visible, was probably that constructed on the spot where the Great Basilica was sunsequently raised. It is visible now only by series of ruined walls projecting form below the church, and a public water fountain on the line of the main entrance street from the bridge. This bath was fed directly by the city's aqueduct.

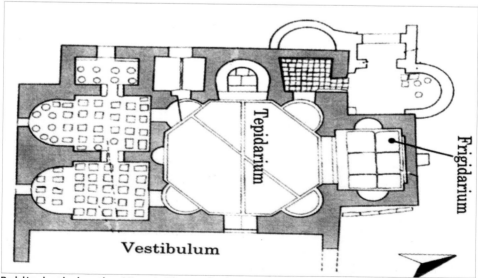

Public bath by the Vivari Channel plan

Public bath-house by the Vivari Channel

Tepidarium

Frigidarium

Caldarium

Public bath-house by the theater and its plan

Public bath-house by the Baptistery and its plan

Public bath-house by the
Great Basilica

The Triconch Palace

So far few domestic buildings have been excavated in the city, though the numerous small baths suggest there were many. The Triconch Palace is one of a number of elaborate later Roman town houses known from around the Mediterranean, but unlike the Triconch of Butrint few have been excavated to modern standards. Such houses generally date from the 4th century AD, and none seem to have been built after AD 530. In its initial phases, in the 2nd to 4th centuries, the Triconch was a modest residence with wings and a peristyle arranged around a stone-flagged pavement and a well, which can be seen in the centre of the excavated area. There were two entrances, one from the west into the peristyle and another from the east into the long gallery of the southern range. This latter was intended as a high-status access perhaps taking the most important guests form a private landing stage into the heart of the house. An extremely fine mosaic composed of interlocking decorative bands and panels with theatre masks emphasise the status of this entrance as well as the cultural level of the owners. Many of the other rooms were paved with mosaics; one in the original entrance hall contained a Greek inscription that gives some information about the owner. Despite the building's modest dimensions, the owner, whose name is only partially preserved, is referred to in the mosaic inscription as 'clarissimus', a rank that would have given him the status of senator. So here we have the dwelling of one of Butrint's leading citizens, probably a member of the city council.

Around AD 425, there was a massive expansion of the Triconch. A new plot of land to the east was acquired, and the whole building recast as a very grand town house with a big central peristyle, a marine entrance from the channel to the south, with fine views, and another entrance and audience hall leading directly from the city side. The focal point of this new complex was the eastern wing where a large three-apsed *triclinium* (dining room) was built. Elaborate banquets were an important aspect of elite social interaction in Late Antiquity, and it is in these rooms that such events were staged, the diners reclining on special semicircular dining couches, known as *stibadia*. The place of honour was on the left as you approached, and the guests were positioned in descending order of rank until on the right was the man known as the parasite, invited for his wit and in order to be the butt of jokes. While the central apse ranked first, three apses permitted the provision of three couches, and numerous diners. The central space was for servants and entertainers.

The Triconch Palace was almost completed, the columns and tiled roofs set up, and the carved stone windows (with Christian motifs) installed when work stopped. Why the complex was abandoned at this time is unknown – only later was the palace separated from the Vivari Channel by construction of the new city wall, which runs across the south side of the site. The abandoned complex was robbed of its stone and turned over to industry, with workshops housed in wooden shacks, and later it was used as a cemetery. However, the location remained a good one and as Butrint's fortunes improved in the Middle Ages, timber buildings were erected amongst the ruins. The earliest of these dates from the 9th century, and domestic and other activity continued well into the 13th century. Many of these apparently ephemeral timber structures were, in fact, substantial dwellings, outbuildings and workshops in the shadow of the city walls. After this the site of the former Triconch Palace was used only sporadically, and finds of 16th-century pot sherds and 19th century gunflints and shotgun cartridges are the only trace of the hunters who stalked game amongst the trees at the water's edge.

To the west of the Palace site, is another complex, the so-called Merchant's House, with buildings arranged around a small open area. The complex has a similar history to that of the Triconch Palace, but with a difference: it was by and large a commercial facility, with warehousing and a yard where boats could be drawn up, and it continued to be used after the 6th century, long after the palace was abandoned. When the city wall was erected a special water gate was provided to allow fisherman and merchants to unload their cargoes. The warehouses were surmounted by second-storey dwellings in the 6th century, presaging the medieval concept of wealthy houses with living space over shops, workshops or byres. Much of Butrint's water frontage must have been arranged similarly, with wealthy houses interspersed with port facilities and workshops.

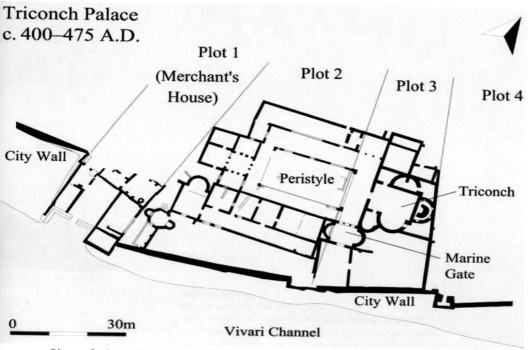

Triconch Palace
c. 400–475 A.D.

Plot 1
(Merchant's House)

Plot 2

Plot 3

Plot 4

City Wall

Peristyle

Triconch

Marine Gate

City Wall

0   30m

Vivari Channel

Plan of the Trichonch Palace

Aerial view of the Trichonch Palace

The Trichonch Palace

Mosaic
in the
Trichonch
Palace

Remains of a Venetian house

Remains of a Venetian mill

Christian buildings

The Acropolis Basilica

Built probably in the 5th century the acropolis basilica was placed on the very highest point of the city, perhaps on the site of a temple. The church was built with a nave and two aisles, a narthex and at the eastern end a triconch presbytery. Much of this has bow collapsed over the edge of the acropolis ghill and the resue of the building as a medieval foritifcaiton has left it a confused tangle of walls. There was also a series of mosaics which were largely removed or destroyed during early excavations.

The Great Basilica

The church survives almost up to roof height, making it one of the best-preserved late antique basilicas in the region. It has a central nave with clerestory, aisles and transepts of tripartite form, separated from the nave and *bema* by pilasters. The apse is of polygonal form, originally with three large windows. Contrary to the findings of previous surveys, it now appears that the structure of the church is substantially original, and that the arcades were always carried on rectangular piers, not columns. Notable on the western piers by the apse are the scored marks of the masons who erected the church, a series of crosses cut into the grouting mortar to ward off the evil eye. Of the original decoration, only a fragment of the mosaic floor of the *bema* now survives, together with some patches of plaster on the interior walls and piers. In the apse stand some fragments of marble altar screens, which would have decorated and subdivided the nave.

A church like this would have been divided internally into a hierarchy of spaces, with the *bema* (the space in front of the apse) and main nave being the most important areas reserved for the priests. In the Great Basilica of Butrint the *bema* floor is covered by mosaic, and the nave with stone slabs. The aisles were for the general congregation and so would usually be paved less elaborately. The transepts could be for the use of the clergy or perhaps for wealthy patrons who paid for and frequented the building, permitting them close proximity to the altar. In the centre of the nave is the foundation for an *ambone* or pulpit, with twin stairs, which would have played an important part of the ceremonies that took place in the church.

Despite its size and elaboration, the Great Basilica was not Butrint's episcopal church in Late Antiquity: for one thing, it contains burials - burial was not permitted in episcopal churches for several centuries to come. Moreover, fragments of the elaborate marble decoration of another grand church have been found elsewhere around Butrint, so the episcopal seat of late antique Butrint remains to be discovered. The great basilica itself appears to have been a funerary church, or perhaps even a shrine containing martyrs' relics, which travellers would pass by and visit on their way into the city.

The Medieval Churches

A series of other churches in the city of Butrint belong to the Middle Ages. Those are the small church near the baptistery with its typical Epirote bell tower, one above the Lake Gate, asmall Byzantine chapel with the very fragmentary remains of frescoes within, and the churches near the western and southern walls of the acropolis all built in the 13th and 14th centuries. Traces of the mural paintings can still be seen in these churches.

The Baptistery

This is one of Butrint's key monuments and one of the largest and most elaborate baptisteries of its time anywhere in the Mediterranean. The construction of the baptistery can be dated from a stylistic analysis of the great mosaic pavement, which belongs to the period c. AD 550–575. The complex was built over the remains of a Roman bathhouse, the form of which dictated the size of the circular central space. The double ring of eight columns (the Christian number of perfection) would have supported arcades that in turn held up the domed roof. A high lantern over the font would have allowed light to shine down on this central feature, while another window was set in the eastern wall, opposite the door. Other windows may have been set into the walls, above the benches on which the initiates, or catechumens, would have sat.

The baptistery's main feature today is the great mosaic pavement. In Late Antiquity it would have been equally conspicuous, as the walls and vaults of the interior of the building most likely would have been less richly embellished. The mosaic is a remarkable composition: its principal scheme is based on seven concentric bands, two of which consist of plain interlocking medallions, containing roundels with animals, 69 in total, a variety of quadruped creatures and many water birds and fish – all symbols associated with baptism. The other bands include interlaced patterns and an outer framing band of vine leaves. Inside the main door, opposite the eastern window and the small fountain below, are three principal figurative panels: a pair of fighting cockrels, to ward off evil; an elaborate scene of two peacocks, the symbols of paradise, perched in a vine, the tree of life, which sprouts from a *kantharos* cup, symbolising communion; and beyond this, next to the font, two cypress trees flanking a cross, from the foot of which flow two streams, the water of life, from which deer drink, symbolising the cleansing of the soul through the waters of baptism. And a reference to the biblical psalm: *Like the hart desireth the water–brooks, so longeth my soul after thee, O God.*

The building was the setting for the elaborate and highly important baptismal rite. In Late Antiquity Easter Sunday was the only day of the year on which baptism could take place. On Easter Sunday morning, the bishop would process with his clergy and the initiates to the Baptistery, just as light was breaking over the rooftops of the city and shining through the eastern window. The procession would enter the building, the catechumens seating themselves on the benches while the bishop and his assistants took their positions. One by one the catechumens would be summoned to the font, down into which they would step, before having water poured over them, an act known as effusion. Stepping out of the font the initiates were symbolically reborn. They were robed in white before proceeding through a door into the next room. This adjacent space also has a mosaic floor, somewhat cruder than that of the central space but seemingly donated by a bishop of the city, to judge from a fragmentary inscription in the floor. Here the newly baptised would have waited before processing en masse to the cathedral church to receive first communion. The baptistery was equipped with a small hypocaust to heat and purify water in a copper tank for use in the baptism. Its remains can be seen on the southeast corner of the outside of the building.

The Necropolis

In Butrint, there are two identified necropoles, one Hellenistic and the other Roman. The Hellenistic necropolis is situated ont he western side of the city, outside the surrounding walls, on the isthmus. The fnds form these grave were not very rich, mainly pottery and bronze objects of 3rd –2nd centuries BC. The necropolis was reused in the roman period.

The Roman necropolis is far more extensive, coivering the same area as he Hellenistic cemetery but extending up onto the hillside, all along the Vivari channel, on the northern side of the city, where tombs are visible by the Lion gate, and also onto the Vrina Plain.

Hellenistic building

In the vicinance of the Lake Gate and the surrounding walls, are preserved the ruins of a building which is dated in the 2nd century AD. It is compounded of two ambient, a room (9.20 x 6 m) and another room leading to the first one (3.40 x 2.65 m), another space of 3.40 x 3.20 m and a corridor of 1.70 m long.

Map of the Medieval Churches

Aerial view of the Great Basilica

The Great Basilica, 5th century AD

Plan of the
Great Basilica

53

The Acropolis Basilica 5th century AD and its plan

Church of the Baptistery,
9th – 10th century AD

Church of the Scean Gate,
9th – 10th century AD

Roman bath-house

Baptistery

Mosaics

2nd century
4th-5th century
6th century
13th-14th century

Plan of the Baptistery

Aerial view of the Baptistery

Byzantine Capitol

57

The archaic temple
in the Acropolis

The Roman necropolis

Hellenistic building, 2nd century BC

The Venetian castle and Acropolis

The summit of the acropolis offers fine views over the Vrina Plain to the south. The conical mountain of Çuka e Ajtoit is visible in the distance, and further on is Konispoli, close to the border with Greece. To the west is a fine view down the Vivari Channel, with Corfu in the distance. At the head of the channel the ruins of the castle of Ali Pasha can be seen, a fortress constructed by the Pasha at the end of the Napoleonic wars to protect Butrint from outsiders, notably the British, then in occupation of the Ionian islands. Since that time, the acropolis has been the scene of more recent political events. The Soviet leader Nikita Khrushchev visited in 1959. The castle in the Acropolis was begun by h Byzantines, then used by the Angenin's during their occupation, but much of the rpesent masonry seems to be Venetian. In fact the whole acroplis suummit comprised the caslte, the enclosed area seen today is a pastiche created by the Italian Archaeologicla Mission of the 1920s and 30s. They took some of the remains of the 'palace' of the late Medeival Captain of Butrint and converted them into the single sizable tower and the circuit walls and courts to be seen today. built by the Venetians, following the lines of the archaic fortification. The archaeological museum of Butrint is located inside.

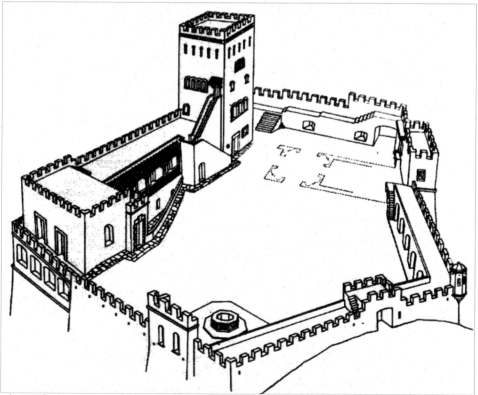

Plan of the reconstruction of the Acropolis castle (after Ugolini 1930)

The tower of the Venetian castle

The Venetian Castle and Acropolis

Kalivo

Kalivo is a rocky hill on the southern shore of Lake Butrint. Up to about 5,000 years ago, the hill appears to have been virtually surrounded by the waters of the lake, which have gradually receded over the course of the last three millennia as alluvial material has been washed down the valley by the River Pavllas. Even during the last 2000 years it is likely to have been separated from the dry land of the plain by wide river channels. On its northern side there is an extremely steep slope down to the lake, while the east, south and west sides are more gently sloped but nevertheless difficult to climb. A circuit of walls encompasses the east, south and west sides of the hill. This is built from small, rough polygonal blocks. The eastern wall has a neatly constructed north tower or bastion, built on a square plan overlooking the lake. Three gates survive in the circuit, two on the east side and one on the south, the latter being the most impressive, with a narrow passage and masonry standing to 3 m in height. Other sections of the wall on the eastern side are equally impressive. The wall has never been securely dated, and suggestions range from 12th century BC, during the Bronze Age, to the 5th century BC, or the Iron Age. Excavations in the 1930s, 1950s and in 2004 have all attempted to resolve this problem but the question remains open. Within the walls there are the remains of dry-stone or earth-bonded structures. On the high point of the hill stands a masonry-built enclosure containing a number of buildings, one of which is of considerable size. Excavations here have revealed roughly tiled floors and ceramics, including terracotta figurines, dating from the 3rd century BC, suggesting that this is the remains of a Hellenistic-period farmstead or even a rustic sanctuary. On the eastern and southern slopes, survey work has revealed similar dry-stone buildings, surviving to only one or two courses in height and seemingly organised in a regular pattern. Elsewhere, ceramics of Roman and medieval production have been found on the hilltop. On the western slopes, outside the line of the wall circuit, are the remains of a Roman brick-built vaulted tomb.

Kalivo remains something of an enigma. It may have formed the nucleus of a proto-urban Hellenistic settlement before Butrint developed as a city. It seems to have played some role in the Roman settlement pattern and may have been reoccupied in the post-Roman period.

Fragment of the fortification wall in Kalivo

Aerial view of the fortification in Kalivo, 12th century BC

A Gate in Kalivo

Diaporit

This site is located on the southeast shore of Lake Butrint, close to the sites of Butrint and Kalivo. The site was first discovered by the Italian Archaeological Mission in the inter-war period, but has more recently been the subject of extensive excavations as part of an Anglo-Albanian programme of research excavations at Butrint. The site comprises three main phases of occupation. The first phase consists of a large villa complex in a fine location overlooking the lake. This complex has been dated to the 3rd century BC, though only a few wall foundations have so far been identified. The second phase of the villa dates to the Roman imperial period (1st century AD, with 2nd-3rd century additions) when it was reoriented to face Butrint on the opposite shore of the lake. The most substantial remains surviving today, the upstanding corner of a polygonal room of the bathhouse, and a number of excavated terrace and building walls, belong to this complex, the function of which changed from residential to industrial in the 3rd century AD. Thereafter the complex was largely abandoned.

Diaporit is one of a number of villas in the immediate hinterland of Butrint. Evidence from tile stamps suggest that this complex may well have belonged to a client family of Titus Pomponius Atticus, the friend and correspondent of the orator Cicero, who owned lands near Butrint in the later 1st century BC.

The final phase corresponds with the reoccupation of the villa complex in the late 5th and 6th centuries AD. At this time a basilica and associated buildings were constructed on one of the upper terraces. The outline of the church is perfectly visible, with a narthex, nave and aisles. The floor of the nave was paved with tiles, and the aisles appear to have had clay floors, so despite its architectural complexity it was not elaborately decorated. To the south lie the remains of what appears to be a small villa-style building, or perhaps an early monastery, with its own chapel, a minute bathhouse, and a tower, possibly a bell tower. The remains of the earlier Roman buildings were turned over to domestic use. The site has been dated through stratified finds, and together with the Vrina Plain excavations represents the only Roman villa and early Christian basilica site in all of Albania and northern Greece to be excavated using stratified archaeological techniques.

A number of graves of the same date as the Diaporit monastery were found cut into the ruins of the Roman villa. Interestingly, many of these contained the remains of women, suggesting that the community here may have been a convent. It is not unlikely that the later buildings belonged to a small monastery, typical of the many that were founded by groups of monastic pioneers or farsighted landowners in Late Antiquity. The community at Vivarium (Squilace) in southern Italy, founded by Cassiodorus, the minister of the Ostrogothic king Theoderic the Great, is the most famous of these in western Europe.

Basilica of Diaporit

Aerial view of Diaporit

The public bath-house and the Roman villa, Diaporit

The Vrina Plain

Excavations here have uncovered substantial sections of a quarter of Butrint established in the Roman period. Geophysical surveys have revealed ranges of buildings across an area of some two hectares, and it is clear that the land was centuriated, or organised into regular square plots. This was a typical feature of Roman colonies, in this case the colony established by Augustus, though other cities used similar systems. Nevertheless, the earliest buildings that have been identified out on the plain date to the mid-1st century AD. They consist of a number of separate structures that seem, by the later 1st century, to have been consolidated into a single complex, a substantial Roman villa, perhaps with two peristyles and various reception and living quarters. Excavation within the walled enclosure has revealed a central garden with a large and elaborate brick-built fountain and pool, surrounded by porticoes and ranges of rooms and, to the north, a sizeable apsed room, probably a reception hall.

The 1st-century complex subsequently underwent major alterations and was probably abandoned by the mid- to late 3rd century AD. Later, in the 4th century, the site was reoccupied and a basilican building erected. By the 5th century this was certainly being used as a churhc. The church's fine mosaic floor survives, depicting the creatures of the creation: animals of the earth, sea creatures and birds arranged in a series of square panels. The *bema* and apse of the aisled building were separated from the nave by a screen. A substantial narthex was laid out to the north, with an external exonarthex, or outer entrance vestibule, possibly giving access from a private landing stage.

By the 9th century the basilica had fallen out of use and an aristocratic dwelling constructed above it. The discovery of a series of lead seals (including one from a eunuch of the bedchamber of the Great Palace of Constantinople), which originally accompanied official documents, attests to the resident commander's administrative role, and to the Vrina Plain manor house as one of the central points for the Byzantine organisation of the Butrint area. Kilns, ovens and furnaces surrounding the building also point to it being a productive centre. Burials of the 10th and 11th centuries, in the nave and outside the apse of the former church, contained very high-status metalwork and horse fittings. The apse and bema area seems to have continued to be used as a small chapel. The entire complex was abandoned by the 13th century.

Other work has been done on the plain in addition to this excavation. Elsewhere, ~~so far~~ the principal discovery has been that of a small temple possibly dating to the 2nd century AD. The Temple faced the major north-south road that led via the bridge into Butrint. Behind it was the line of the city aqueduct, a single pier of which can be seen behind the Temple. The Temple is of the Italic type, raised on a concrete podium some 2 m high. A brick-built cella was fronted by a *pronaos* with up to six Ionic columns, and a central staircase led down to the road. The whole was clad in stone. This building may be a particular type of sacred structure known as a *heroon*, or hero shrine, the focus of the funerary cult and may have been the mausoleum associated with the villa. The remains of marble sarcophagi and human bones found in the cella lend weight to this idea. Like the Roman dwelling described above, the Temple seem to have gone out of use by the mid-3rd century AD.

Mosaic of the Basilica in the Vrina Plain

Beyond the temple are various other monuments. A single standing cremation tomb, with a tower-like superstructure and its vault intact, is all that can be seen of a major cemetery that covered a large area of the Vrina Plain. Interestingly, the cemetery seemingly was interspersed with villas in the area extending towards Kalivo. To the south are three brick-built piers of the aqueduct, with the springing of the arches still visible.

Aerial view of the Basilica in the Vrina Plain

Aerial view of the Temple

Butrint
Museum

Apolloni, shek. IV p.Kr

Butrint Museum

The Butrint Museum was built in the 1950s to house the finds of the Italian archaeological mission that first excavated in Burin from 1928 to 1940.

Between 1960 and 1980 Albanian archaeologists continued these excavations and in 1988 the museum was enlarged to introduce the history of the antique city throughout the ages.

In the summer of 2005, the museum was renovated and updated, enriched this time by the joint excavations undertaken by the Albanian Institute of Archaeology and the Burin Foundation since 1994.

The museum was re-opened in 2005 thanks to the support of the Albanian Institute of Archaeology, the Burin Foundation, the A. G. Dementis Foundation, the Packard Humanities Institute and the Burin National Park.

Early occupants and the changing environment

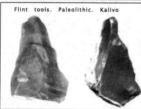

Flint tools. Palaeolithic and Mesolithic. Xarra

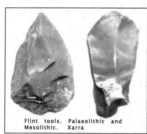

Flint tools. Paleolithic. Kalivo

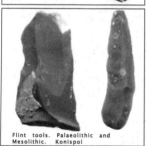

Flint tools. Palaeolithic and Mesolithic. Konispol

Flint tools. Palaeolithic and Mesolithic. Shën Mitri

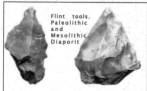

Flint tools. Paleolithic and Mesolithic. Diaporit

18,000 years ago the landscape around Burin was very different from today. Sea levels were much lower and Corfu was joined to the mainland. 9,000 years ago, the sea rose and the hills that you now see around you, like Xarra, Shëndëlli, Kalivo and Shën Dhimitri, became small islands. Since then rivers and rain have carried silt and clay from the mountains to the coast and what was once sea has slowly become salt marsh, and later, dry land.

The discovery of stone tools on these former islands demonstrates that the area has been occupied since prehistoric times.

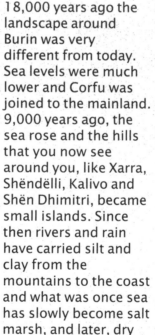

Decorated lid vessel. Neolithic

Cup. Neolithic

Pottery fragment. Neolithic

Painted pottery fragments. Neolithic

Decorated pottery fragments. Middle Neolithic

Bone tools. Neolithic

The Butrint region in the Bronze and Iron Ages

From 1200 BC, the area around Butrint was inhabited by tribes who lived in hilltop settlements. These were often steep–sided and fortified, suggesting that the tribes frequently lived in a state of insecurity and conflict. Butrint itself seems to have started as one of these tribal settlements.

Bronze Age. sites around Butrint

Bowl. 1800-1500 BC

Prehistoric walls at Butrint

Prehistoric walls at Cape Stillo

Ritual pots. 1800-1500 BC

Local two-handled pots 1800-1500 BC

Local one-handled pot. 1800-1500 BC

Local two-handled pots 1800-1500 BC

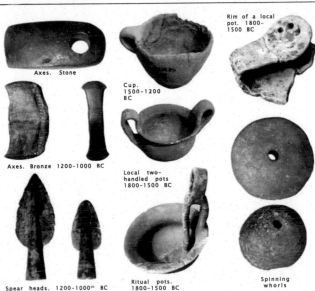

Axes. Stone

Axes. Bronze 1200-1000 BC

Spear heads. 1200-1000th BC

Cup. 1500-1200 BC

Local two-handled pots 1800-1500 BC

Ritual pots. 1800-1500 BC

Rim of a local pot. 1800-1500 BC

Spinning whorls

Aeneas flees Rome (Federico Barocci, 1598, Villa Borghese, Rome)

The origins of Butrint

According to legend Butrint was founded by the Trojan exiles Helenus and Andromache after the fall of Troy in the 13th century BC. In the epic poem "The Aeneid", Virgil writes of Aeneas visiting the exiles at Butrint on his way to Italy. While there is archaeological evidence from the 12th century BC, Butrint didn't flourish as a settlement until the 8th century BC. Excavations on the acropolis have revealed quantities of imported 8th century pottery from Corinth, which shows that Butrint was part of an important network of Mediterranean trade and culture.

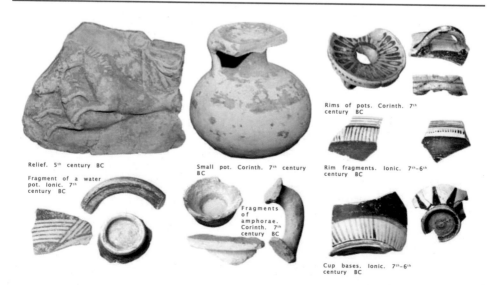

Relief. 5th century BC

Fragment of a water pot. Ionic. 7th century BC

Small pot. Corinth. 7th century BC

Fragments of amphorae. Corinth. 7th century BC

Rims of pots. Corinth. 7th century BC

Rim fragments. Ionic. 7th–6th century BC

Cup bases. Ionic. 7th–6th century BC

Hellenistic Butrint, 3rd century BC

Hellenistic Butrint

By the 4th century, perhaps on account of its natural springs, the settlement of Butrint had become a religious site dedicated to the God of healing, Asclepius. This was a time of growth for Butrint when a complex of sanctuary buildings, hostelries and meeting places was built for the priests and the pilgrims. The theatre was used for religious purposes as well as for dramas and public events. A substantial circuit of walls was built around the sanctuary and the acropolis, using the natural defensive qualities of the lake and channel. Much of this wall circuit can still be seen today.

Tableware. 3rd–2nd century BC

Terracotta figurines 3rd–2nd century BC

Cosmetics container. 3rd–2nd century BC

Tableware. 3rd–2nd century BC

Pot. 3rd–2nd century BC

Knife. Iron

Votive vessels. 3rd–2nd century BC

Oil Lamps. 3rd–2nd century BC

Perfume flasks. 3rd–2nd century BC

Phoinike to the north of Butrint

The theatre Phoinike

Defensive walls at Phoinike

Butrint and its religious sanctuary lay in the territory of the Praisabes tribe, who were part of the Chaonians – one of the confederations of people who occupied the region of Epirus.

At this time, the principal town in the region was Phoinike immedia-tely to the north of Lake Butrint. Phoinike played an important role in the rise of King Pyrrhus (318–272 BC), who invaded Roman lands in Italy. His victories against the Romans were so costly, they ultimately led to his defeat and the phrase "Pyrrhic victory".

Phoinike was later conquered by Teuta, Queen of the Illyrians in circa. 230 BC. Subsequently the Romans led by Aemilius Paulus conquered Epirus in 167 BC and enslaved much of its population.

Butrint was spared destruction, possibly because the Romans respected it as a healing sanctuary.

King Pyrrhus

Tableware. 3rd–2nd century BC
Jug. 3rd–2nd century BC
Perfume glass bottle. 3rd–2nd century BC
Pot. 3rd–2nd century BC
Pot. 3rd–2nd century BC
Container for cosmetic use. 3rd–2nd century BC
Urn for infant burial. 3rd–2nd century BC
Amphora. 3rd–2nd century BC

The cult of Asclepius at Butrint

The Sanctuary of
Asclepius, 4th
century BC

Votive objects
dedicated to
Asclepius

Throughout much of its ancient history Butrint functioned as a religious centre dedicated to Asclepius, the god of healing. Visitors would sleep within the precincts of the temple, hoping for a dream or vision that would guide them to a cure for their ailments. Priests and physicians performed rituals to interpret the dreams and supply the medicines prescribed. The Sanctuary attracted visitors from all over the region. They dedicated votive objects to the god Asclepius to hasten their recovery. Many of these votive objects were recovered during the excavation of the sanctuary in the late 1920s.

Other gods were also worshipped at Butrint, including those of Apollo, Artemis Athena, Demeter and Zeus. Some of the dedicatory statues are displayed here

Bust of Asclepius

The Italian excavations around the sanctuary and theatre (1930)

374

 6, 97169842561 153363241821560666799987

(Page 76)

The Economy of Ancient Butrint

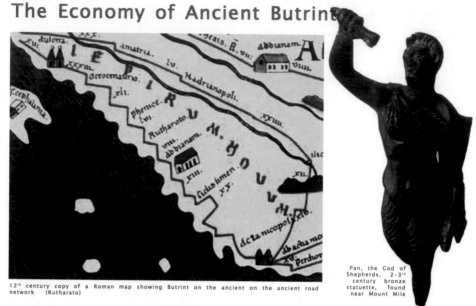

12th century copy of a Roman map showing Butrint on the ancient on the ancient road network (Rutharato)

Pan, the God of Shepherds, 2-3rd century bronze statuette, found near Mount Mile

As well as its role as a cult site, Butrint occupied a strategic position as a gateway into the interior of Epirus. Although the sea was always more important than the land as a means of transport, Butrint was linked to an extensive road network connecting the region.

Archaeological finds demonstrate Butrint's trading links throughout the Mediterranean as well as the presence of local craftsmen such as metal workers and potters.

Over the centuries the inhabitants enjoyed a rich and varied relationship with the landscape, cultivating the terrain, rearing livestock, fishing in the lake and sea and hunting in the surrounding hills. The evidence for these activities survives from many periods showing considerable continuity over the centuries.

Loom weights. 3rd–2nd century BC

Oil lamp mould. 4th century AD

Tiles with inscription. 1st–2nd century AD

Frescoes from the Forum. 1st–2nd century AD

Agricultural tools

Objects for fishing. Bronze

Architectural fragments. 1st–2nd century AD

Stone mortars.

Moulded Hellenistic and Roman pottery. With floral motifs

Manumission – The freeing of slaves

One of the most remarkable finds at Butrint is a series of inscribed stones that record the freeing of slaves in honour of Asclepius. The inscriptions were found in two places first on the wall of the theatre, and second as a series of blocks reused in a later tower. Some examples can be seen here. As well as recording the names of the slave owners, the inscriptions give information about how the region was governed through a complex system of administrative bodies. They also record some of the different gods worshipped at Butrint, with slaves being released in honour of Zeus Sotiris and Pan as well as Asclepius himself.

The inscriptions tell us that the role of women in society here was markedly different from that of Classical Greece. Women were allowed to own and release slaves themselves and in the event of the husband's death, his property passed to his wife, rather than the eldest son.

"Lyso has freed, according to the law of the people without children, Aphrodisia, Aristonika, A—a, Epikrat— who will live with Lyso during her life-time"

An example of a manumission , found at the theatre.

Inscriptions on the wall of the theatre, recording the release of slaves

Detail from the Tower of Inscriptions

Germanicus Julius, son of Tiberius, grandson of Augustus Caesar, consul, elected as [honorary] quinquennal; Caius Julius Strabo, son of Caius, acting as prefect on his behalf. Date: 12 BC

Sacred to Minerva this temple was erected by Octilius Mystes at his own expense on land donated by the city council. Date: 2nd century AD

Lucius Domitius Ahenobarbus, son of Cnaeus, pontifex and consul, honoured by decree of the decurions as patron of the colony. Date: 16 BC

Silver denarius, 83–82 BC, showing the head of Jupiter (found at Butrint) Reverse: the winged goddess Victory in a four-horse chariot

Augustan Bronze coin minted at Butrint, showing the head of a bull Reverse: the tripod of Apollo

Silver denarius showing the Emperor Trajan; AD 103–111 (found at Butrint) Reverse: the goddess Victory holding a wreath and a palm leaf

Money at Butrint

The many coins found at Butrint show the wide range of the city's economic links through the long history of the Graeco-Roman Mediterranean. They include coins minted at Greek cities such as Corinth and Kerkyra (Corfu), as well as coins from the Macedonian and Illyrian regions and Italy.

Of particular interest are those struck at Butrint during the reigns of the Roman emperors Augustus, Claudius and Nero. These coins honoured the town and commemorated the Roman colony of Butrint.

Some coins depict the city's aqueduct while others have an image of a bull which became the symbol of Butrint. Legend describes how the Trojan exile Helenus sacrificed a bull which struggled ashore at Butrint and died. Helenus took this to be a good omen and founded the City "Buthrotum", meaning "bull crossing" in Greek.

Bust of Julius Ceasar (Staatliche Museen zu Berlin)

Bust of Cicero (Capitoline Museum, Rome)

Caesar's Legacy

Shortly before his death in 44 BC, Julius Caesar founded a Roman colony at Butrint which was further developed under the reign of Augustus. For a brief period the people who shaped the future of the Roman world took a personal interest in the town. Their presence and influence is shown in the statues and inscriptions found in the heart of the city.

Much of what we know of Butrint's history in this period comes from the letters of Cicero, the famous Roman politician and orator. Cicero's friend, Atticus, who owned an estate near Butrint, was concerned at the potential loss of land associated with the arrival of the colonists. He pleaded with Cicero to lobby on his behalf to prevent the foundation of the colony. Although Atticus's half of the correspondence is lost, Cicero's letters provide a fascinating insight into the moment when Butrint briefly figured on the political stage of Rome itself.

"Let me tell you that Buthrotum is to Corcyra (Corfu) what Antium is to Rome – the quietest, coolest, most pleasant place in the world."

Cicero Letters to Atticus 4.8.1 (56 BC))

Roman Butrint

Butrinti in the late 1st century AD

The foundation of the colony under Julius Caesar had a major physical impact on the town.

A large section of the city wall was removed for the construction of a forum, the great open space that formed the heart of the Roman town. Public and private buildings of every kind were erected – fountains, baths, gymnasia and prominent funerary monuments – and statues of the imperial family were displayed in the theatre and other public spaces.

The late 1st century AD was a prosperous period for Butrint and its inhabitants. The citizens enjoyed a high standard of living with fine glass and tableware being common in many house-holds.

Flask. 1st–2nd century AD

Toilet bottle. 1st–2nd century AD

Small container and vessel lid for cosmetic use. Bone

Window glass. 2nd–3rd century AD

Finger-rings. Copper alloy. Early Roman

Flask. 2nd century AD

Oil lamps. 2nd–3rd century AD

Bust of Silenius. Roman

Head of a young man. Roman

Head of a young man. Roman

Head of a young man. Roman

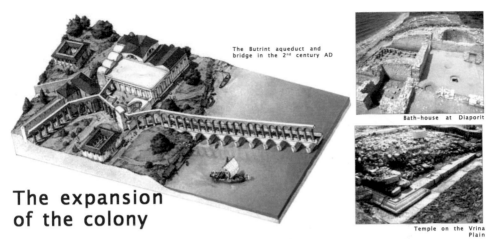

The Butrint aqueduct and bridge in the 2ⁿᵈ century AD

Bath-house at Diaporit

Temple on the Vrina Plain

The expansion of the colony

Recent excavations of the Roman colony suburb, across the channel on the Vrina Plain, have revealed the prosperity of Butrint in this period. An aqueduct along with a bridge was constructed to connect the old town to the new suburb on the plain. The suburb was laid out along a regular grid of streets. Houses and public buildings fronted the channel and at its centre stood a prominent temple, the site of a major cult.

At Diaporit, on the far shore of Lake Butrint, a great private villa stood on a series of terraces, with large rooms and garden-walks overlooking the lake. We know that Titus Pomponius Atticus would have lived in a villa like this somewhere in the area.

Huge amounts of amphorae and table wares have been discovered here, showing trade connections from both the western and eastern Mediterranean, oil from Spain, fine table wares from Tunisia and Asia Minor, wine from Italy, Crete and Syria, and cooking pots from the Aegean.

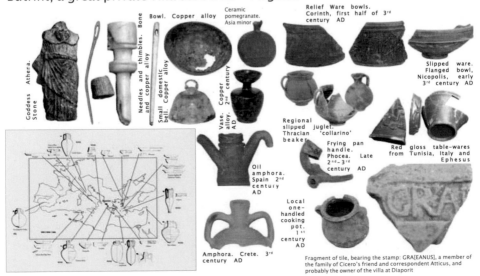

Goddess Athera. Stone

Needles and thimbles. Bone and copper alloy

Bowl. Copper alloy

Small domestic bell. Copper alloy

Ceramic pomegranate. Asia minor

Vase. Copper alloy. 2ⁿᵈ century AD

Relief Ware bowls. Corinth, first half of 3ʳᵈ century AD

Slipped ware. Flanged bowl, Nicopolis, early 3ʳᵈ century AD

Regional slipped juglet. Thracian 'collarino' beaker

Frying pan handle. Phocea. Late 2ⁿᵈ–3ʳᵈ century AD

Red gloss table-wares from Tunisia, Italy and Ephesus

Oil amphora. Spain 2ⁿᵈ century AD

Local one-handled cooking pot. 1ˢᵗ century AD

Amphora. Crete. 3ʳᵈ century AD

Fragment of tile, bearing the stamp: GRA[EANUS], a member of the family of Cicero's friend and correspondent Atticus, and probably the owner of the villa at Diaporit

Early Roman Butrint (2nd century AD)

Piers of the aqueduct, Vrina Plain

Late Roman Butrint (6th century AD)

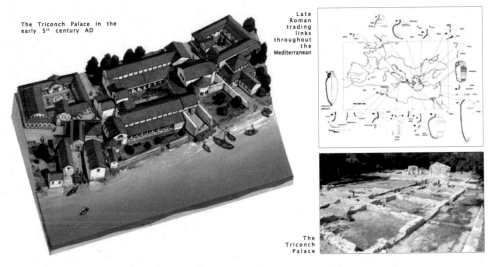

The Triconch Palace in the early 5th century AD

Late Roman trading links throughout the Mediterranean

The Triconch Palace

Butrint in the late Roman Mediterranean

The late Roman period saw a new wave of urban developmental Butrint, best demonstrated by the Triconch Palace, a grand residence belonging to a senator and one of the town's leading citizens. Elegant rooms were ranged around a courtyard cooled by a fountain and later a magnificent clover-leafed banqueting hall was added along with a water gate for visitors.

In the later 5th century Epirus suffered from devastating Vandal raids. The ordered life of the city changed dramatically and houses became simpler and smaller with upper storeys constructed of wood. In the 6th century, agricultural activity took place in the ruins of the buildings, and the dead were sometimes buried within the fallen walls. The health of the population was poor, and their skeletons show signs of disease.

Despite these changes, it is clear that Mediterranean trade flourished and the Butrint had access to goods now primarily from North Africa and the eastern Mediterranean.

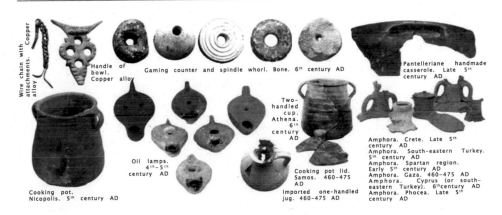

Wire chain with Copper attachments. alloy

Handle of bowl. Copper alloy

Gaming counter and spindle whorl. Bone. 6th century AD

Pantelleriane handmade casserole. Late 5th century AD

Two-handled cup. Athena. 6th century AD

Oil lamps. 4th–5th century AD

Cooking pot lid. Samos. 460–475 AD

Imported one-handled jug. 460–475 AD

Cooking pot. Nicopolis. 5th century AD

Amphora. Crete. Late 5th century AD
Amphora. South-eastern Turkey. 5th century AD
Amphora. Spartan region. Early 5th century AD
Amphora. Gaza. 460–475 AD
Amphora. Cyprus (or south-eastern Turkey). 6th century AD
Amphora. Phocea. Late 5th century AD

The 5th century church built above the ruins of the Roman villa at Diaporit

Reconstruction of the 5th century church, Diaporit

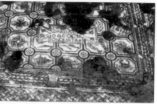

Mosaic from the basilica, Vrina Plain, with an inscription describing the church donors:
"Those whose names God Knows"

Christianity and social change

The first mention of a Christian presence concerns the martyrdom of St Terinus who was reportedly thrown to the beasts in an ampitheatre at Butrint sometime between AD 249–251. Many prominent early Christian buildings were constructed at Butrint, including the Baptistery and the Great Basilica, in particular during a short period between the late 5th and the mid 6th century. Other churches have recently been discovered in the new Roman town on the plain and at the earlier Roman villa of Diaporit. In this period, Christian symbols were commonly incorporated on objects of every kind, alongside other magic devices, to protect their owners from malevolent spirits and the dangers of everyday life.

The cultural changes that took place as the power of the Roman state dwindled, are apparent in the new social structures and the changing fashion in dress and personal ornaments.

Leaf-shaped object. Copper alloy

Hanging lamp bracket. 6th century

Pendant with cross. Lead. 5th century

Brooch in the form of a pelta shield. Copper alloy

Architectural terracotta showing Gorgon's head

Ampula for holy oil from the shrine of St. John, Ephesus. 6th century

Container for holy oil from the shrine of St.John, Ephesus. 6th century

Plate with crosses. Phocean red-slip ware. 6th century

Oil lamps with crosses 5th–6th century

Plaque with a hunting dog leaping the evil eye. Bone. 4th century

Cretan amphora with infant burial. Found Triconch palace. Early 6th century.

Fragments of altar screen. Late 5th century

Peacocks with vase and vines symbolising salvation and paradise

Affronted cocks symbolising resurrection

Stags drinking from a stream, a reference to the 42nd psalm.

Wading birds, the faithful saved through baptism

Fish, representing sinners saved by Christ

The baptistery mosaic

Rabbit eating grapes, the faithful saved through the Eucharist.

Flowers in bloom, plant of Paradise

The baptistery mosaic

Re-erecting the baptistery columns, 1930

The Baptistery mosaic

The mosaic of Butrint's Baptistery is the largest and most complete of any baptistery in the Roman world. It was designed to send clear messages of salvation and everlasting life to those who chose to be baptised. Around two concentric rings of eight columns, seven rings of mosaic surround the central cruciform font, making another sequence of eight. For early Christians the number eight symbolised baptism, new creation and salvation.

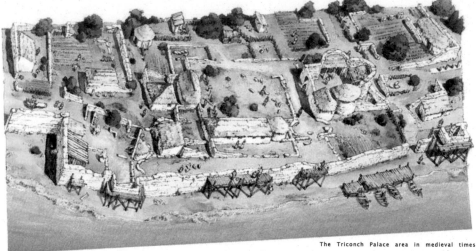

The Triconch Palace area in medieval times

Byzantine Butrint

We know very little of Butrint for the period following the mid-7th century. The town reappears in historical sources in the late 9th century. In 1081 Butrint was briefly taken by the Normans and the bay was the scene of a great sea battle between the Norman and Byzantine fleets. The Arab geographer, Ibn al Idrisi, reported that Butrint was well populated in the 12th century, although Benedict of Peterborough described it as a "deserted castle" in 1191.

Gold coin of the Byzantine emperor Basil II, found at the Triconch Palace.

During the 13th century Butrint thrived again. A castle was built on the acropolis and the wall around the channel-side was repaired. Several churches survive from this time and finds of amphorae and glazed pottery from Italy and the Aegean demonstrate renewed trading contacts. Houses were usually made of wood, sometimes built on the foundations of earlier Roman buildings.

Proto-Maiolica bowls from S. Italy. Mid-13th/mid-14th century

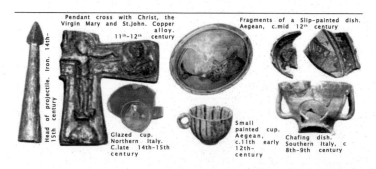

Head of projectile. Iron. 14th-15th century

Pendant cross with Christ, the Virgin Mary and St.John. Copper alloy. 11th–12th century

Fragments of a Slip-painted dish. Aegean, c.mid 12th century

Glazed cup. Northern Italy. C.late 14th-15th century

Small painted cup. Aegean, c.11th early 12th century

Chafing dish. Southern Italy, c 8th-9th century

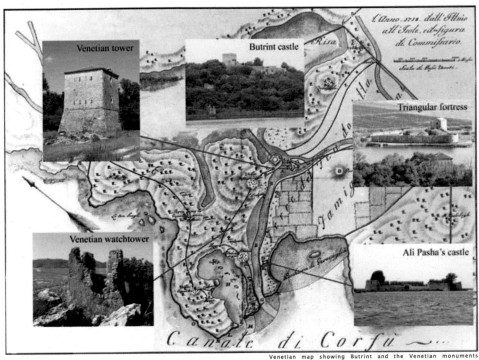

Venetian map showing Butrint and the Venetian monuments

Dining habits in the Venetian and Ottoman periods

During the 15th–16th centuries, people living in Butrint were eating from decorative glazed dishes and bowls, mostly imported from Northern Italy and Venice.

Hoard of Bronze coins. Found during excavations at the Triconch palace, 12th century, Byzantine.

Hoard of bronze coins of the Angevin period, 13th century

Hoard of Venetian silver coins, 14th century

Venetian Butrint

The Venetians purchased Butrint from the Angevin kings of southern Italy with the island and fortress of Corfu, in 1386. For the next four hundred years the garrison was never more than an outpost of Corfu, sometimes referred to as Corfu's 'protector and right eye'. Its fisheries provided a substantial proportion of Corfu's diet, and the plains to the south of the Vivari Channel were ideal for pasturing the livestock and the horses of Corfu's garrison.

There were many repairs to the fortifications of both the lower town and the acropolis. Eventually in 1572 the defences of the town were abandoned in favour of the Triangular Castle that guarded the Vivari Channel. The Castle was besieged on a number of occasions.

Ali Pasha

By the start of the 19th century, Butrint had dwindled in size and was no more than a fishing village, clustered around the Triangular Castle. The settlement belonged to AN Pasha, who ruled Epirus from his castle at Ioannina.

Sometimes known as the Muslim Bonaparte, Ali Pasha was a ruthless ruler who brought prosperity to the region by building roads and a network of strong fortresses.

Lake of Butrint

The French diplomat Pouqueville described him in 1806: The extreme suppleness of the motions of his countenance, the fire of his little blue eyes, impressed on me the alarming idea of deep cunning, united with ferocity".

Butrint was a favoured hunting destination for Ali Pasha. He built the present castle that can be seen at the mouth of the Vivari Channel. In 1820, Ali Pasha was dismissed from his offices and he was murdered at Ioannina a year later.

Ali Pasha, painted on a hunting expedition at Lake Butrint by Louis Dupré (1819)

VIVARI CANAL

Ali Pasha's castle, Vivari Channel

"Butrinto, Albania", by Edward Lear, 1861, (Yale Center for British Art)

Early Tourists

From the late 18th century foreign diplomats and Grand Tourists such as Lord Byron were regular visitors to Ali's court, and it was they who began to write of the ancient remains of Butrint.

The Aga's house", by Henry Cook (c.1850)

In 1825, the French painter, Louis Dupré, visited Butrint and wrote that"... one day, exploration of the ruins will bring forth a great wealth of discoveries that have been covered for all these centuries by the curtain of night".

The great British painter, Edward Lear made many sketches of Butrint in 1857 and in the 1850s Henry Cook, a British lithographer, drew the ruins by the Channel. Seventy years later, Gerald Durrell, the celebrated naturalist, recalled childhood memories of hunting in the Butrint marshes in *My Family and Other Animals*.

"Butrint", by De la Poer Beresford (c. 1855)

Corinthian amphora, 6th century BC

Pithos, 2nd–3rd century AD

Roman amphora, 1st–2nd century AD

Late Roman ampora

Byzantine amphora

Medieval amphora

Statue of Artemis, goddess of the hunt. Found during the excavations at Phoenic 1962-27. 3rd-1st century BC

Statue of Artemis, goddess of the hunt. Found during the excavations at Phoenic 1962-27. 3rd-1st century BC

Statue of Artemis, goddess of the hunt. Found during the excavations at Phoenic 2003-4.3rd-1st century BC

Statue of Dionysius, god of wine. Found during excavations in the nymphaeum at Butrint1929. 2nd century AD

Statue of Apollo, good of sun. Found during excavations in the nymphaeum at Butrint1929. 2nd century AD

Statue of a Muse. Copy of the imperial Period of a Hellenistic original

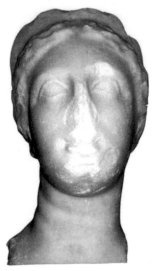

Head of Demeter, wife
of Pluto King of the
underworld. 3rd–1st
century Bc

Head of Aphrodite, the
goddess of love.
Found at Phoenice.
1st century AD

Head of Aphrodite, the
goddess of love.
First centuriesnof the
Roman period

Portrait of Augustus
who became the first
emperor after the defeat
of Mark Anthony and
Cleopatra at Actium,
south of Butrint in 31
BC. Found during the
theatre excavations
Butrint 1928. Last
quarter of the 1st
century BC

Portrait of Empress
Livia, wife of Augustus.
Found during the
theatre excavations
Butrint 1928. Last
quarter of the 1st
century BC

Portrait of Marcus
Vipsanius Agrippa, the
great general of
Augustus and the victor
of Actium. Found
druing excavations at
the 'tower of
inscriptions' at Butrint
in the 1980s. Last
quarter of the 1st
century BC

Portrait of Empress
Livia, wife of
Augustus.Found druing
the theatre excavations
Butrint 1928.
Last quarter of the 1st
century BC

Statue of woman.
Found in the shrine of
Asclepius 1930
Hellenistic

Statue of a muse.
Found in the shrine of
Asclepius during
excavation 1931.
Roman

Bust of Antinous, lover of
Emperor Hadrian, and a
controversial figure who
drowend while travelling with
the emperor in Egypt. Found
during excavations near the
theatre Butrint in the
1960s.c.130–140 AD

Byzantine
capital

Relief representing the healing god
Asclepius seated. Found in 1938
near the Hellenistic tower gate
Butrint. 3rd–1st century BC

Marble funerary caket for
cremation burials. Found in the
western cemetery at Butrint.
Roman

A window from the Triconch
Palace.

Statue and Head of Berenike,
wife of Pluto King of the
underworld 3ˢᵗ century BC.

Marble relief depicting Nike,
4ᵗʰ century BC

Statue of a man,
3rd-2nd century BC

Statue of Augustus from the
2002 excavation in the Forum

Togate statue from the 2005
excavation in the Forum

Togate statue from
theexcavation in the
temple of Aesculapius

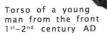

Portrait statue of Agripina

Body of the "large Herculaneum Type"

Statue of Apollo, god of sun

Endimioni, 2ⁿᵈ century AD

Fragment of a statue with "hermaic pilaster" (Hermes, the messenger of gods)

Torso of a young man from the front 1ˢᵗ–2ⁿᵈ century AD

Jonic capital, 4ᵗʰ century BC

Female torso from the Front, 1ˢᵗ–2ⁿᵈ century AD

Vista aerea di Butrinto

BIBLIOGRAPHIE

Baçe, A.   Baths dating from the first Century AD. Monuments, 19, 1980

Budina, Dh.   Butrint Necropolis. BUSHT, 2, 1959. Archeological Map of
                the Ionian Coasts and Delvina Basin. Illyria, 1, 1971.

Cabanes, P.   Les inscriptions du theatre de Boutrotos. Annales litteraires
                de l'Univerite de Besancon, 1974. L'Empire de la mort de
                Pyrros a la conquete romaine, Paris, 1976.

Ceka, N.   Ancient Fortification of Buthrotum and the Prasaebes
                Territory. Monuments, 12, 1976.
                Buthrotum. Tirana 2002.

Crowson, A.   Venetian Butrint. Butrint Foundation, 2007.

Çondi, Dh.   Butrinti. Tirane, 1983
                Villa-fortress at Malathrea. Illyria, 2, 1984
                Archaeological Excavation at Vrina Plain. Buthroti,
                Tirane, 1988
                Aquaduct in Vrina Plain and the city. Illyria 1-2, 1999-2000

Drini, F.   On the Political Institutions in the Prasaebes Koinon.
                Illyria, 1, 1986

Drini, F.   Newly Founded Inscriptions in Butrint. Illyria, 1, 1981
Budina, Dh.

Gilkes, O.J.   The Theatre at Butrint. British School At Athens, 2003.

Gilkes, O.J.   An Italic Style Temple from the Vrina Plain at Butrint.
Çondi, Dh   Illyria, 2009

Hamond N.G.L Epirus. Oxford, Oxford University Press, 1967.

Hansen, I.L.   Roman Butrint. Oxford, Oxbow Books, 2007.
Hodges, R.

Henandez, D. Excavation of the Roman Forum at Butrint. USA, JRA, 2008.
Çondi, Dh

Hodges, R. Eternal Butrint. A Unesco World Heritage Site in Albania.
London, General Penne Publishing
Saranda, Ancient Onchesmos. A short History and Guide.
Tirana, Migjeni

Hodges, R. Byzantine Butrint. Excavations and Surveys 1994–99.
Bowden, W. Oxford, Oxbow Books.
Lako, K.

Karaiskaj, Gj. Butrint and its Fortifications. Tirana, 1983.

Meksi, A. Butrint Big Basilica and Baptistery. Monuments, 1, 1983

Mitchell, J. The Butrint Baptistery and its Mosaics.
Butrint Foundation, 2008

Mitchell, J The Early Christian Basilica on the Vrina Plain.
Greenslade, S. CANDAVIA, 2, 2007
Leppard, S.
Çondi, Dh.

Nanaj, A. Protourban Buthrotum. Illyria, 1985.

Ugolini, L.M. Butrinto. Il mito d'Enea, gli scavi. Rome, Instituto Grafico
Tiberino.
Albania Antica III, L'Acropoli di Butrinto. Roma, 1942.